Color Your Life!
A Kid's Guide To Lisbon, Portugal

Photography By John D. Weigand
Poetry By Penelope Dyan

Bellissima Publishing, LLC
Jamul, California
www.bellissimapublishing.com

copyright © 2012 by Penny D. Weigand & John D. Weigand

All rights reserved. No part of this book may be
reproduced or transmitted in any form or by any means,
electronic or mechanical, including photocopying,
recording, or by any other means, or by any information or
storage retrieval system, without permission from the publisher.

ISBN 978-1-61477-030-5
First Edition

"I don't paint things the way I see them, but the way I think them."

PABLO PICASSO 1881-1973

Color Your Life!

Bellissima Publishing, LLC

Introduction

When you get to Lisbon, Portugal, the first thing you notice is all the color and contrast. It is as though there is a pallet of color set before your eyes like a fine old painting. Award winning author, attorney and former teacher, Penelope Dyan, was struck with this concept. More important even than the museums was the color that seemed to pop out at her; and she felt that this was not only what a child would notice, but it was also a perfect opportunity to show them the art of the streets where they could call out the colors gleefully. Dyan believes a place is always more about what you see with your eyes and feel in your heart. A place can tell you about the people in the way even the simple streets present themselves. This is not to say that visiting a museum is not something unimportant, and our travelers do show you some of those. It is simply that you need to see through the eyes of your child, and try to see what they see and then build upon that--everything you do and every place you go can be a new, wonderful lesson--and you don't even have to work very hard to teach that lesson if you tune into a few key things, things to make a kid think and create and become excited about what it means to learn! This book is not filled with boring facts. This book is filled with purpose as are all the Dyan/Weigand travel books---purpose and fun!

Color Your Life!
Bellissima Publishing, LLC

Color Your Life!
A Kid's Guide To Lisbon, Portugal

Photography By John D. Weigand
Poetry By Penelope Dyan

As you go down the streets of
Lisbon you pass this wall,
a picture of buildings
standing colorfully tall.
This mosaic of tiles mimics
the colors of the street.
And it all reminds you
life is terribly sweet.
And as you hold
your mother's hand,
she whispers to your father,
"Isn't life grand!"

There is an ancient Roman
aqueduct in Lisbon
that you can see,
serving as an example of now
and of how things USED to be,
when ancient people came
from Rome,
to call Lisbon, Portugal
their home sweet home.

The buildings on the streets
are colorful against the
blue hues of the skies.
You stop and you look,
and you rub your little eyes.
In fact, here you simply
look and look;
because the street looks
like a storybook!

You never thought you liked museums filled with with art; but in this modern museum, the Berardo Museum,* you don't know where to start! Your mom shows you a Picasso. Then you smile. Picasso has your kind of style! There's an eye painted here, a smile painted there. . . and lots of color everywhere!

*The Berardo Museum has one of the world's most acclaimed modern art collections, with works by Warhol, Picasso, Dali, Duchamp, Magritte, Miró, Bacon, Jackson Pollock, Jeff Koons, among others representing dozens of modern movements.

There's a suspension bridge
set against the blue of the sky.
You stare in awe
and take a picture
as you walk slowly by.
A statue of Christ stands arms
opened wide.
He welcomes visitors from the
Tagus River's side.*

*The 25 de Abril Bridge (the "25th of April Bridge") is a suspension bridge connecting the city of Lisbon, capital of Portugal, to the municipality of Almada on the left (south) bank of the river. The statue of Christ was built in 1959 in thanks to God for having spared Portugal during WWII. The monument was inspired by the famous statue in Rio de Janeiro.

There's a building, a restaurant!
Flowers bloom in window boxes.
You see ornate tiles of green.
It is one of the most
interesting places to eat
that you have ever seen.
Mom and Dad ask,
"Do you want to get something
here to eat?"
You say, "Yes," and go inside;
and then have something sweet.

There's a bright orange house!
(Family laundry hangs outside.)
It's warm, and the windows
are open wide--
They're waiting for the cool
breezes to begin. . .
and to bring the fresh, dried
laundry in!

You get really excited.
Mom says you're going to look
at the night sky,
to study the all the stars
twinkling up on high.
And to make things even
oh so more right,
it's a planetarium,
so there's no wait for tonight.
Mom says that soon you will see
just how beautiful the stars
(without all the smog) can be!

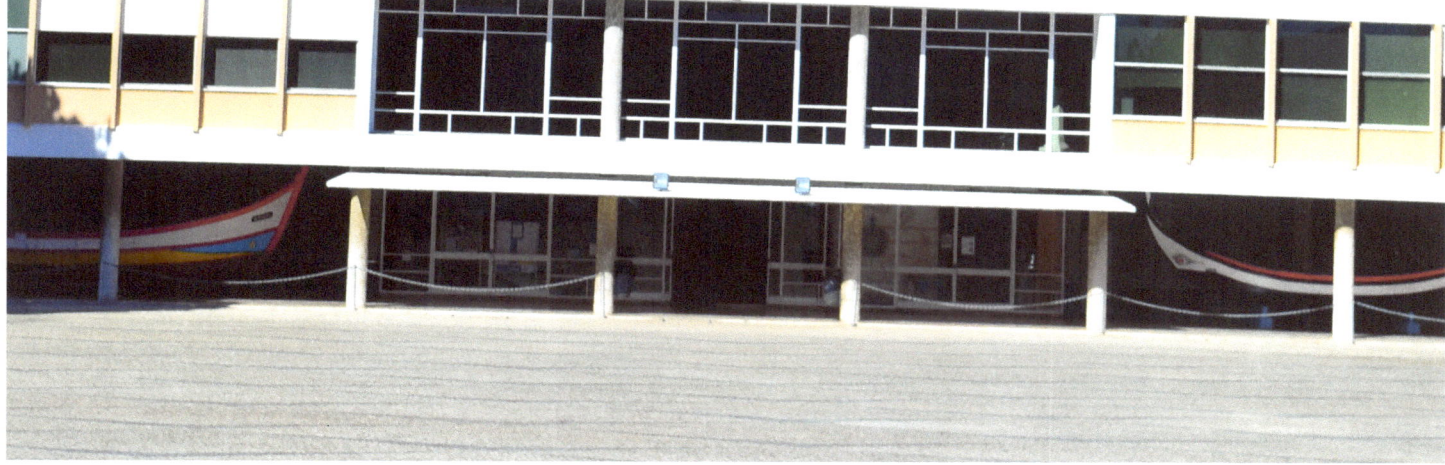

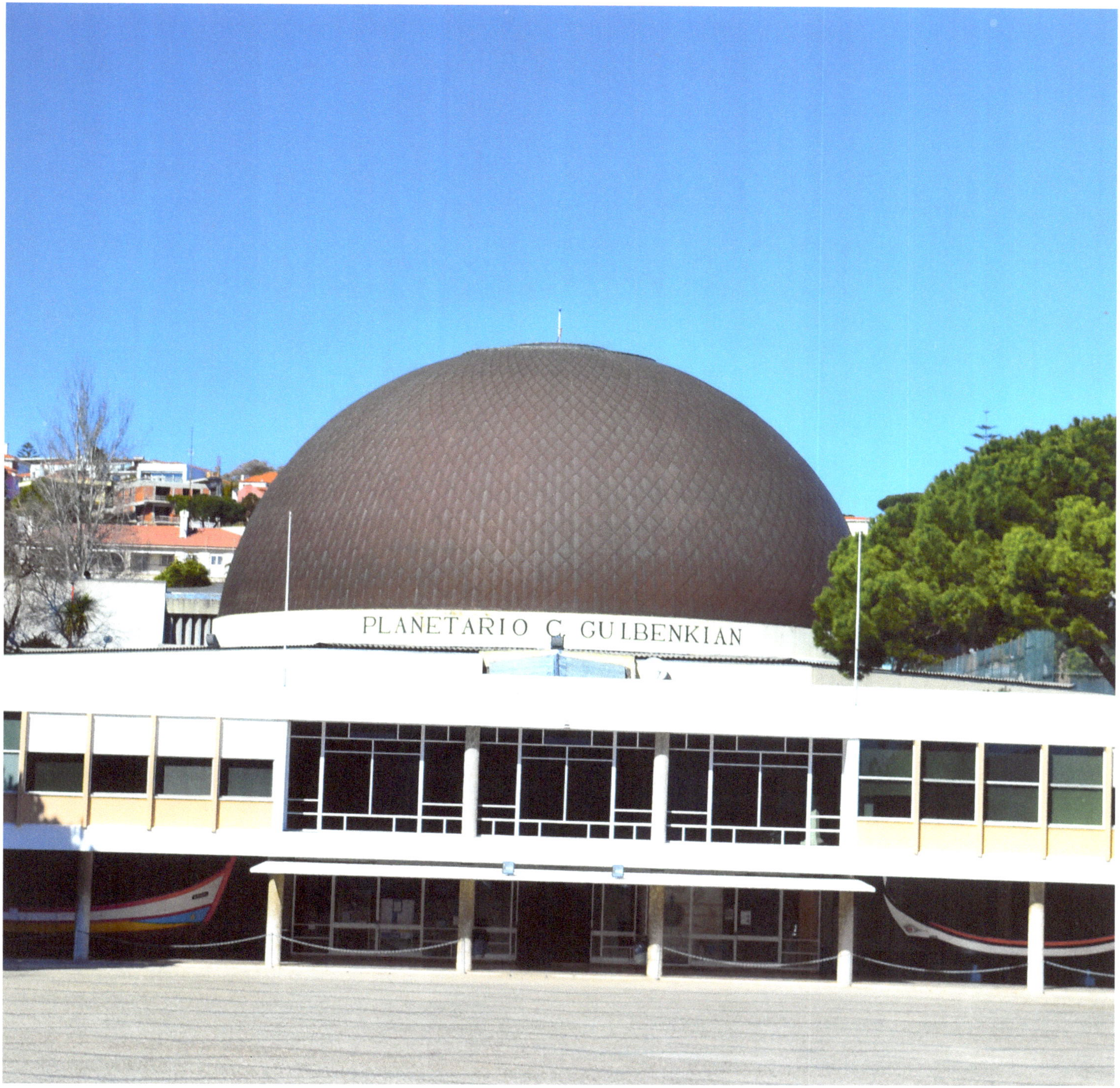
PLANETARIO C. GULBENKIAN

Here is a place built in the
1800's where you do
not want to stay,
not for a week
or for even one day.
This colorful place is the
Main Lisbon Prison,* you see;
and it's definitely NOT where
YOU want to be!

*The Main Lisbon Prison was built in 1874. and is still used today.

The Belém Tower looks like a castle and makes your imagination and YOU run wild. Mom says, "Please calm down." (But you ARE still a child.) There it is! A ceremonial gateway, once used as a prison, you are told.
Built in the 16th century means it's VERY, VERY old!*

*Belém Tower (in Portuguese Torre de Belém,) or the Tower of St Vincent is a fortified tower located in the civil parish of Santa Maria de Belém in the municipality of Lisbon, Portugal. The tower was commissioned by King John II to be part of a defense system at the mouth of the Tagus River and a ceremonial gateway.

There's an old yellow trolly
in front of a building
as bright as the sun.
You all decide to hop on board,
because it looks like
lots of fun!
across the square and town
and up the street you go!
You think it's lots fun,
even IF it's rather slow.

There's an old biplane.
The Belém Tower's behind.
You run around on the grass.
Dad takes pictures of the find!
You imagine you're a pilot
flying high up in the sky.
Dad says, "You can be
anything you want to be!
All you have to do is TRY!"
You go to your hotel, eat, and
go to bed; and upon a pillow
soft, you rest your weary head.

*Visits always give pleasure
- if not the arrival, the departure.*

~ Portuguese Proverb

Printed in the USA
CPSIA information can be obtained
at www.ICGtesting.com
LVHW060259150224
771926LV00002B/9